Write, Heal, Thrive:
A Transformative Journaling Experience

Write, Heal, Thrive:
A Transformative Journaling Experience

Written by Melissa B. Lombardo
Illustrations by Eduardo José Arias Cruz

Copyright Notice

Contact

For permission requests, quantity sales, special discounts, production and licensing assistance, speaking engagements, and workshops, contact the author at: info@melissablombardo.com

Publisher's Cataloging-in-Publication Data

Write, Heal, Thrive: A Transformative Journaling Experience

Written by Melissa B. Lombardo. First Edition

    1. Self Help.

    2. Personal Transformation, Sexual Abuse.

    3. Women

Illustrations by Eduardo José Arias Cruz. *eduardoariascruz.com*

Author portrait by Alicia Ann Daw

Styling by Jessica Dutton

Layout, cover design, and Write, Heal, Thrive logo designed by Nikita Prokhorov. *nikitaprokhorov.com*

Copy editing by Peter J. Lombardo, K. Leigh Wright Riser, Maureen Cody Carroll

Printed in the United States of America

Publisher information: Write, Heal, Thrive, West Hartford, CT

ISBN 979-8-9877587-2-4 (paperback)

Publisher Note

The information presented should not serve as legal or medical advice. The author does not assume responsibility for actions or non-actions taken by individuals who have read, written, or used the materials contained within this publication. No person shall be entitled to any claim for the contents of the works, information or statistics provided, or views expressed in this publication. The author and publisher are not responsible for external websites and their content.

This published work is designed to provide information regarding the subject matter. It is sold with the understanding that neither the publisher nor the author is rendering psychological, legal, or other services. Neither the publisher nor the author is held liable for any actions or results accrued from this book, journal, or performance piece. If expert assistance including counseling is needed, please seek the counsel of a professional. Readers are advised to do their own due diligence when it comes to making decisions.

Hurt, Healing, and Hope: Thriving beyond Sexual Assault; a dynamic book and performance piece delivering a collection of interwoven monologues detailing true stories of hurt and healing post-sexual assault, child abuse, domestic violence, and its 100% aftereffects.

"Sharing individual experiences, and showing their similarities and differences, will hopefully inspire others facing the trauma of sexual assault to believe that there can be healing and hope after the life-changing hurt, and everyone's journey is their own. My drive to write is inspired by an ever-increasing desire to help others, to light the way to what's possible and truly within reach. I credit writing as one of the reasons I was able to heal. I founded "Write, Heal, Thrive" based on the inspiration that writing became a way for me to heal, and through healing, I moved from hope into thriving, something I continue to do each day."

-Melissa B. Lombardo, Author, Speaker, Advocate

CONTENTS

Dedication

To the countless journals I have written in and to those who gifted them to me.

To each of you writing in this sacred space.

Introduction

Journaling can be therapeutic for inner healing. Processing through journaling and writing may help overcome stress, anxiety, and other overwhelming emotions. I love that journaling has no rules. I can write about whatever I choose...good, bad, or ugly; I do not fear judgment about my self-expression.

I have kept a journal since I was 12 years old and continue to do so today. In the months and years after the trauma of sexual assault, journaling took on new significance as an integral part of my healing process. My then counselor at the local sexual assault crisis center urged me to write down my feelings using writing prompts and drawing my emotions. Journaling gave me a chance to write freely and organize my thoughts about the assault in a way that made sense to me. As time went on, I felt empowered to reclaim my narrative. My personal journey through trauma unfolded through writing. My journal became a safe space that fostered healing as I explored many emotions and reactions to one of the most difficult times in my life.

Many years later those journal entries formed a basis for what became a collection of interwoven monologues published as a book and performance piece titled, "Hurt, Healing, and Hope: Thriving beyond Sexual Assault." At the time I never could have imagined how journaling the events of my past would help open me to further healing, restore my physical health, and find my authentic voice.

It is my hope that the book and this journal may help guide you to achieve additional healing from your own traumatic experience. I commend your courage in the steps you are taking and wish you well on your journey.

In writing and healing,

How to use this journal

You may use the following lined pages on which to record your thoughts while gaining inspiration from gentle self-care reminders and writing prompts dispersed throughout the book.

It is nice to be reminded of our worth. Gentle self-care reminders are included at the bottom of the journaling pages to provide you with a short piece of advice, inspiration, motivation, and introspection. You may read them in the order they are listed, turn them into your own personal affirmation statements, or choose a new at random that resonates with you each day of your healing journal.

Writing prompts are at the beginning of the journal section for inspiration to get you started. You may want to choose a writing prompt one day and then free-write a different day. The choice is yours.

Due to the sensitivity of this topic, emotions may arise before, during, and after journaling, and you may be unsure how to handle them. Reaching out for support can help. You may choose a trusted person to talk to or you can contact your local 24-hour Crisis Center for immediate assistance. Help is always available. I encourage you to reach out to others if you feel you need additional support.

Journal

How do you feel about yourself today, at this present moment?

_____

_____

_____

_____

_____

_____

_____

_____

_____

_____

_____

_____

_____

_____

_____

_____

_____

_____

_____

_____

_____

_____

_____

_____

_____

_____

_____

_____

_____

_____

_____

_____

_____

_____

_____

_____

_____

_____

_____

_____

_____

_____

_____

_____

_____

_____

_____

_____

_____

Date_____

Write an encouraging letter to your body.

_____

_____

_____

_____

_____

_____

_____

_____

_____

_____

_____

_____

_____

_____

_____

_____

_____

_____

_____

_____

_____

_____

_____

_____

_____

_____

_____

_____

_____

_____

_____

_____

_____

_____

_____

_____

_____

_____

_____

_____

_____

_____

_____

_____

_____

_____

_____

_____

_____

_____

_____

_____

Write about how you matter to the world and those around you.

_____

_____

_____

_____

_____

_____

_____

_____

_____

_____

_____

_____

_____

_____

_____

_____

_____

_____

_____

_____

_____

_____

_____

_____

Date_____

Write about ways in which you can nourish yourself: mind, body, and soul.

_____

_____

_____

_____

_____

_____

_____

_____

_____

_____

_____

_____

_____

_____

_____

_____

_____

_____

_____

_____

_____

_____

_____

_____

_____

_____

_____

_____

_____

Date_____

Today I am grateful for...

_____

_____

_____

_____

_____

_____

_____

_____

_____

_____

_____

_____

_____

_____

_____

_____

_____

_____

_____

_____

_____

_____

_____

_____

_____

_____

Describe what gives you a sense of safety and security.

_____

_____

_____

_____

_____

_____

_____

_____

_____

_____

_____

_____

_____

_____

_____

_____

_____

_____

_____

_____

_____

_____

_____

_____

_____

_____

_____

_____

Date_____

Write about how you want to begin feeling.

_____

_____

_____

_____

_____

_____

_____

_____

_____

_____

_____

_____

_____

_____

_____

_____

_____

_____

_____

_____

_____

_____

_____

_____

_____

Date_____

_____

_____

_____

_____

_____

_____

_____

_____

_____

_____

_____

_____

_____

_____

_____

_____

_____

_____

_____

_____

_____

_____

_____

_____

_____

_____

_____

_____

Create positive healing affirmations to repeat to yourself in difficult moments.

_____

_____

_____

_____

_____

_____

_____

_____

_____

_____

_____

_____

_____

_____

_____

_____

_____

_____

_____

_____

_____

_____

_____

_____

_____

_____

_____

_____

_____

_____

_____

_____

_____

_____

_____

_____

_____

_____

_____

_____

_____

_____

_____

_____

_____

_____

_____

_____

_____

_____

_____

_____

_____

_____

_____

_____

_____

_____

_____

_____

_____

_____

_____

_____

_____

_____

_____

_____

_____

_____

_____

_____

_____

Be kind to yourself.

_____

_____

_____

_____

_____

_____

_____

_____

_____

_____

_____

_____

_____

_____

_____

_____

_____

_____

_____

_____

_____

_____

_____

_____

_____

Write your story, even if it is only for you.

_____

_____

_____

_____

_____

_____

_____

_____

_____

_____

_____

_____

_____

_____

_____

_____

_____

_____

_____

_____

_____

_____

_____

Your story matters. You matter.

_____

_____

_____

_____

_____

_____

_____

_____

_____

_____

_____

_____

_____

_____

_____

_____

_____

_____

_____

_____

_____

_____

_____

Self-care is important to help with healing.

_____

_____

_____

_____

_____

_____

_____

_____

_____

_____

_____

_____

_____

_____

_____

_____

_____

_____

_____

_____

_____

_____

Write with your heart.

Write from your heart.

_____

_____

_____

_____

_____

_____

_____

_____

_____

_____

_____

_____

_____

_____

_____

_____

_____

_____

_____

_____

_____

Writing takes courage.

_____

_____

_____

_____

_____

_____

_____

_____

_____

_____

_____

_____

_____

_____

_____

_____

_____

_____

_____

_____

_____

_____

_____

Writing is speaking out.

_____

_____

_____

_____

_____

_____

_____

_____

_____

_____

_____

_____

_____

_____

_____

_____

_____

_____

_____

_____

_____

_____

_____

_____

Writing is a way to take ownership.

_____

_____

_____

_____

_____

_____

_____

_____

_____

_____

_____

_____

_____

_____

_____

_____

_____

_____

_____

_____

_____

_____

_____

_____

_____

_____

Remember to rest.

_____

_____

_____

_____

_____

_____

_____

_____

_____

_____

_____

_____

_____

_____

_____

_____

_____

_____

_____

_____

_____

_____

_____

Life and healing are not linear.

_____

_____

_____

_____

_____

_____

_____

_____

_____

_____

_____

_____

_____

_____

_____

_____

_____

_____

_____

_____

_____

_____

_____

_____

_____

Your message is important.

_____

_____

_____

_____

_____

_____

_____

_____

_____

_____

_____

_____

_____

_____

_____

_____

_____

_____

_____

_____

_____

Your feelings are valid.

_____

_____

_____

_____

_____

_____

_____

_____

_____

_____

_____

_____

_____

_____

_____

_____

_____

_____

_____

_____

_____

_____

There is strength in your story.

_____

_____

_____

_____

_____

_____

_____

_____

_____

_____

_____

_____

_____

_____

_____

_____

_____

_____

_____

_____

_____

_____

_____

Take care of yourself.

_____

_____

_____

_____

_____

_____

_____

_____

_____

_____

_____

_____

_____

_____

_____

_____

_____

_____

_____

_____

_____

_____

_____

Writing is one of many ways to heal.

_____

_____

_____

_____

_____

_____

_____

_____

_____

_____

_____

_____

_____

_____

_____

_____

_____

_____

_____

_____

_____

_____

Healing is possible.

_____

_____

_____

_____

_____

_____

_____

_____

_____

_____

_____

_____

_____

_____

_____

_____

_____

_____

_____

_____

_____

_____

_____

Each journey is unique.

_____

_____

_____

_____

_____

_____

_____

_____

_____

_____

_____

_____

_____

_____

_____

_____

_____

_____

_____

_____

_____

_____

_____

Forgive yourself.

_____

_____

_____

_____

_____

_____

_____

_____

_____

_____

_____

_____

_____

_____

_____

_____

_____

_____

_____

_____

_____

_____

This experience does not define you.

_____

_____

_____

_____

_____

_____

_____

_____

_____

_____

_____

_____

_____

_____

_____

_____

_____

_____

_____

_____

_____

_____

Your story needs to be shared.

_____

_____

_____

_____

_____

_____

_____

_____

_____

_____

_____

_____

_____

_____

_____

_____

_____

_____

_____

_____

_____

_____

_____

_____

_____

_____

_____

_____

_____

May you find your own path.

_____

_____

_____

_____

_____

_____

_____

_____

_____

_____

_____

_____

_____

_____

_____

_____

_____

_____

_____

_____

_____

_____

_____

_____

You are a survivor.

_____

_____

_____

_____

_____

_____

_____

_____

_____

_____

_____

_____

_____

_____

_____

_____

_____

_____

_____

_____

_____

_____

_____

You are here.

_____

_____

_____

_____

_____

_____

_____

_____

_____

_____

_____

_____

_____

_____

_____

_____

_____

_____

_____

_____

_____

_____

You are brave.

_____

_____

_____

_____

_____

_____

_____

_____

_____

_____

_____

_____

_____

_____

_____

_____

_____

_____

_____

_____

_____

_____

_____

_____

Your truth is yours alone.

_____

_____

_____

_____

_____

_____

_____

_____

_____

_____

_____

_____

_____

_____

_____

_____

_____

_____

_____

_____

_____

Accept where you are right now.

_____
_____
_____
_____
_____
_____
_____
_____
_____
_____
_____
_____
_____
_____
_____
_____
_____
_____
_____
_____
_____
_____
_____
_____
_____
_____

Hold a safe space for your feelings.

_____

_____

_____

_____

_____

_____

_____

_____

_____

_____

_____

_____

_____

_____

_____

_____

_____

_____

_____

_____

_____

Take small steps, baby steps.

Date_____

_____

_____

_____

_____

_____

_____

_____

_____

_____

_____

_____

_____

_____

_____

_____

_____

_____

_____

_____

_____

_____

_____

One thought at a time.

_____

_____

_____

_____

_____

_____

_____

_____

_____

_____

_____

_____

_____

_____

_____

_____

_____

_____

_____

_____

_____

_____

_____

_____

You are capable of so much.

_____

_____

_____

_____

_____

_____

_____

_____

_____

_____

_____

_____

_____

_____

_____

_____

_____

_____

_____

_____

_____

_____

Your trauma does not define you.

_____

_____

_____

_____

_____

_____

_____

_____

_____

_____

_____

_____

_____

_____

_____

_____

_____

_____

_____

_____

_____

_____

You are not defined by your past.

_____

_____

_____

_____

_____

_____

_____

_____

_____

_____

_____

_____

_____

_____

_____

_____

_____

_____

_____

_____

_____

_____

_____

_____

Just write, don't worry about editing.

_____

_____

_____

_____

_____

_____

_____

_____

_____

_____

_____

_____

_____

_____

_____

_____

_____

_____

_____

_____

_____

_____

Identify your support system allies.

_____

_____

_____

_____

_____

_____

_____

_____

_____

_____

_____

_____

_____

_____

_____

_____

_____

_____

_____

_____

_____

_____

_____

_____

Be gentle with yourself.

_____

_____

_____

_____

_____

_____

_____

_____

_____

_____

_____

_____

_____

_____

_____

_____

_____

_____

_____

_____

_____

Take a break and be with nature.

_____

_____

_____

_____

_____

_____

_____

_____

_____

_____

_____

_____

_____

_____

_____

_____

_____

_____

_____

_____

_____

_____

_____

_____

Notice your feelings.

_____

_____

_____

_____

_____

_____

_____

_____

_____

_____

_____

_____

_____

_____

_____

_____

_____

_____

_____

_____

_____

Healing takes time.

_____

_____

_____

_____

_____

_____

_____

_____

_____

_____

_____

_____

_____

_____

_____

_____

_____

_____

_____

_____

_____

_____

_____

_____

Healing is different for everyone.

_____

_____

_____

_____

_____

_____

_____

_____

_____

_____

_____

_____

_____

_____

_____

_____

_____

_____

_____

_____

_____

_____

_____

This is your journey.

_____

_____

_____

_____

_____

_____

_____

_____

_____

_____

_____

_____

_____

_____

_____

_____

_____

_____

_____

_____

_____

_____

_____

You matter.

_____

_____

_____

_____

_____

_____

_____

_____

_____

_____

_____

_____

_____

_____

_____

_____

_____

_____

_____

_____

_____

_____

Let this be your time to process.

_____

_____

_____

_____

_____

_____

_____

_____

_____

_____

_____

_____

_____

_____

_____

_____

_____

_____

_____

_____

_____

_____

_____

_____

You are here...in this moment,
in your body, in this world.

_____

_____

_____

_____

_____

_____

_____

_____

_____

_____

_____

_____

_____

_____

_____

_____

_____

_____

_____

_____

_____

_____

You have come so far.

You are special.

_____

_____

_____

_____

_____

_____

_____

_____

_____

_____

_____

_____

_____

_____

_____

_____

_____

_____

_____

_____

_____

Take breaks when necessary.

_____

_____

_____

_____

_____

_____

_____

_____

_____

_____

_____

_____

_____

_____

_____

_____

_____

_____

_____

_____

_____

_____

_____

_____

_____

Writing and reflecting are good ways to process and heal.

_____

_____

_____

_____

_____

_____

_____

_____

_____

_____

_____

_____

_____

_____

_____

_____

_____

_____

_____

_____

_____

_____

Sexual assault is never your fault.

_____

_____

_____

_____

_____

_____

_____

_____

_____

_____

_____

_____

_____

_____

_____

_____

_____

_____

_____

_____

_____

There is hope for your future.

_____

_____

_____

_____

_____

_____

_____

_____

_____

_____

_____

_____

_____

_____

_____

_____

_____

_____

_____

_____

_____

_____

Breathe in, breathe out.

_____

_____

_____

_____

_____

_____

_____

_____

_____

_____

_____

_____

_____

_____

_____

_____

_____

_____

_____

_____

_____

_____

You make the world a better place by being in it.

_____

_____

_____

_____

_____

_____

_____

_____

_____

_____

_____

_____

_____

_____

_____

_____

_____

_____

_____

_____

_____

_____

Someday your healing will help others heal.

Date_____

_____

_____

_____

_____

_____

_____

_____

_____

_____

_____

_____

_____

_____

_____

_____

_____

_____

_____

_____

_____

_____

_____

_____

_____

Your story may inspire others.

_____

_____

_____

_____

_____

_____

_____

_____

_____

_____

_____

_____

_____

_____

_____

_____

_____

_____

_____

_____

_____

_____

_____

_____

There is no timetable to heal.

_____

_____

_____

_____

_____

_____

_____

_____

_____

_____

_____

_____

_____

_____

_____

_____

_____

_____

_____

_____

_____

_____

_____

_____

_____

All journeys are about taking small steps.

_____

_____

_____

_____

_____

_____

_____

_____

_____

_____

_____

_____

_____

_____

_____

_____

_____

_____

_____

_____

_____

_____

Healing takes courage.

_____

_____

_____

_____

_____

_____

_____

_____

_____

_____

_____

_____

_____

_____

_____

_____

_____

_____

_____

_____

_____

_____

_____

_____

_____

_____

_____

Your voice matters.

_____

_____

_____

_____

_____

_____

_____

_____

_____

_____

_____

_____

_____

_____

_____

_____

_____

_____

_____

_____

_____

_____

Reclaim your voice.

_____

_____

_____

_____

_____

_____

_____

_____

_____

_____

_____

_____

_____

_____

_____

_____

_____

_____

_____

_____

_____

_____

_____

_____

Remember to have mindful moments throughout the day.

_____

_____

_____

_____

_____

_____

_____

_____

_____

_____

_____

_____

_____

_____

_____

_____

_____

_____

_____

_____

_____

_____

Step back, admire how far you have come.

_____

_____

_____

_____

_____

_____

_____

_____

_____

_____

_____

_____

_____

_____

_____

_____

_____

_____

_____

_____

_____

_____

_____

_____

The future is not yet written.

_____

_____

_____

_____

_____

_____

_____

_____

_____

_____

_____

_____

_____

_____

_____

_____

_____

_____

_____

_____

_____

_____

_____

Your story represents hope.

_____

_____

_____

_____

_____

_____

_____

_____

_____

_____

_____

_____

_____

_____

_____

_____

_____

_____

_____

_____

_____

_____

_____

_____

Your story is inspiring.

_____

_____

_____

_____

_____

_____

_____

_____

_____

_____

_____

_____

_____

_____

_____

_____

_____

_____

_____

_____

_____

_____

_____

_____

You have power within.

_____

_____

_____

_____

_____

_____

_____

_____

_____

_____

_____

_____

_____

_____

_____

_____

_____

_____

_____

_____

_____

_____

_____

You are limitless. You got this.

Drawing

Artistic expressions such as drawing, painting, and even doodling can become powerful tools supporting not only stress and anxiety reduction but as part of healing. Drawing has been found to be mentally stimulating by opening one's brain to further creative activity. Drawing and doodling play an important role as grounding techniques. Please use the following pages and suggested prompts to draw anything you desire and to achieve greater self-reflection. You may also create your own prompts or just draw what comes naturally to you right now.

Draw how you feel right now and add today's date.

Drawing *(Continued)*

Document a joyful experience you had.

Free draw using crayons because we should feel liberated in our lives to color and create and be imperfect beings.

Drawing *(Continued)*   Date_____

Draw one of the writing prompts from the journal section.

Choose and draw a gentle self-care reminder.

Drawing *(Continued)*   Date_____

Draw or doodle what you are grateful for.

Drawing *(Continued)* Date_____

Drawing *(Continued)*

You have come to the end of this journal but not the end of your healing. If you find journaling and drawing to be helpful, continue to do so regularly. As you continue the process, you may have triggers. Be patient with yourself – healing takes time and is never linear. Have a safety plan for those moments you might need extra processing in the form of a trusted friend, a cup of tea, a walk out in nature, or breathing fresh air.

Perhaps through writing or drawing you have found your own added wisdom, reflected a little deeper, and come to new perspectives and additional paths to healing. Each step is important. Remember to pause and breathe and continue forward. I commend you for all your hard work as you move into the next part of your journey.

In closing, I leave you with one final prompt for your next "Write, Heal, Thrive" journal series,

- Describe what can you do today or in the near future to continue your healing journey.

In healing and thriving,

Additional Resources

The Rape, Abuse, and Incest National Network (R.A.I.N.N.) operates a confidential National Sexual Assault Hotline in the United States of America. You can call 24 hours a day: 1-800-656-HOPE.

Below are additional resources for immediate assistance.

988 Suicide and Crisis Lifeline:
988lifeline.org

National Center for Victims of Crime:
victimsofcrime.org

National Domestic Violence Hotline:
www.thehotline.org

National Teen Dating Abuse Helpline:
loveisrespect.org

Rape, Abuse, and Incest National Network (R.A.I.N.N.)
rainn.org/resources

The Trevor Project: Information, and support for the LGTBQ+ community: *thetrevorproject.org/*

Learn More

It would be great to keep connecting via social media; Facebook, Instagram, and my website: www.melissablombardo.com.
You may also use the hashtags **#hurthealinghopebook** and **#writehealthrive**. Contact me for media appearances, workshops, speaking at your events, assisting in a Hurt, Healing, and Hope: Thriving beyond Sexual Assault live performance and author talk at your school or in your community, or subscribing to my email list.

Learn more at: **writehealthrive.com**.

Facebook: /Melissablombardoauthor

Instagram /Melissablombardoauthor

YouTube: /@MelissaBLombardoAuthor

Goodreads: goodreads.com/MelissaBLombardoauthor

Etsy: etsy.com/shop/WriteHealThrive

Acknowledgments

I continue to write, heal, and thrive because of the support and encouragement offered by family and friends including my parents Janice and Peter, my siblings, Michelle, and Peter, Guayo; whose "title" goes beyond anything I can put into words, my son Andrés, my sister-in-law Megan, and my U.S and Nicaraguan family. I appreciate many friends and work colleagues who are part of my extended family and contributed in some way to the book you hold in your hands: Nikita, a lifelong friend and book layout extraordinaire, Leigh, Vanessa, Alison, Debbie, Alex, Becky, Katie, Erica, Jenny, Brian, two different Jessica's, Maureen, Karianna, Peter, Kevin, Sobeyda, Tina, Nicole, Kate Morgan, Melissa Anne, Randall, Ernesto, José, M.R., a few different Joe's and a Mike; you know who you are, Ana Paula, Cesar, Tania, Adam, Diana, Christine, Dan, Julie, Dennis, Marian, and Jason.

Bernard Kavaler has been especially instrumental in publicity support and press mentorship and I continue to receive ongoing valuable support from Dorothy Holtermann, Clementina Esposito, the Birth a Book writers' group, The CT Alliance of Foster and Adoptive Families, The Green Teahouse, and YWCA New Britain Sexual Assault Crisis Service.

I am thankful and humbled by "Jim" and others like him who crossed my path for a moment in time. You remind me why I am doing the work I am doing and give me the strength to continue my work. If you are reading this and think this may be you...Yes, it is! I am honored we had the opportunity to meet.

Meet Us

Photo credit:
Alicia Ann Daw
Stylist:
Jessica Dutton

Melissa Lombardo

Melissa B. Lombardo is a CT State Certified Sexual Assault Crisis Advocate, speaker, and founder of Write, Heal, Thrive LLC. Her first book, "Hurt, Healing, and Hope: Thriving beyond Sexual Assault" is a book and performance piece delivering a collection of interwoven monologues detailing true stories of hurt and healing post-sexual assault, child abuse, domestic violence, and the after-effects. Each story, told from the first-person point of view, includes perspectives from healing allies offering support to survivors. For more information visit melissablombardo.com.

Photo credit:
Eduardo José Arias Cruz

Eduardo José Arias Cruz

Eduardo José Arias Cruz, Nicaraguan visual artist, art instructor, and graphic designer brings the healing journey to life through these original watercolor illustrations. Eduardo beautifully captures the essence of many emotions felt during the nonlinear healing process post trauma. For more information about Eduardo, visit *eduardoariascruz.com*.

www.ingramcontent.com/pod-product-compliance
Lightning Source LLC
Chambersburg PA
CBHW051632120626
46551CB00014B/2052